GARDENING
CONTEMPLATIONS

REFLECTIONS ON SOWING AND TENDING

The mental health & wellbeing publisher

Great Britain 2020 by Trigger Publishing

Originally published as The Gardener's Companion in Great Britain

2004 by Robson Books

Trigger is a trading style of Shaw Callaghan Ltd

& Shaw Callaghan 23 USA, INC.

The Foundation Centre

Navigation House, 48 Millgate, Newark

Nottinghamshire NG24 4TS UK

www.triggerpublishing.com

Text Copyright © 2020 Trigger Publishing

British Library Cataloguing in Publication Data

A CIP catalogue record for this book is available upon request

from the British Library

ISBN: 9781789562071

This book is also available in the following eBook formats:

ePUB: 9781789562088

Trigger Publishing have asserted their right under the Copyright,
Design and Patents Act 1988 to be identified as the author of this work

Cover design by stevewilliamscreative.com

Typeset by stevewilliamscreative.com

Printed and bound in Great Britain by CPI Group (UK) Ltd,
Croydon CRO 4YY

Paper from responsible sources

CONTENTS

GARDEN TALES

The roses red upon my neighbour's vine
Are owned by him, but they are also mine.
His was the cost, and the labour, too,
But mine as well as the joy, their loveliness to view.
They bloom for me and are for me as fair
As for the man who gives them all his care.
Thus, I am rich, because a good man grew
A rose-clad vine for all his neighbour's view.
I know from this that others plant for me,
And what they own, my joy may also be.
So why be selfish, when so much that's fine
Is grown for you, upon your neighbour's vine.

ABRAHAM L GRUBER, My Neighbour's Roses

Hari and I got into the habit of going to the bibighar, and sitting there in the pavilion, because it was the one place in Mayapore where we could be together and be utterly natural with each other. And even then, there was the feeling that we were having to hide ourselves away from the inquisitive, the amused, and the disapproving. Going in there, through the archway, or standing up and getting ready to go back into the cantonment – those were the moments when this feeling of being about to hide or about to come out of hiding to face things was strongest. And even while we were there, there was often a feeling of preparedness, in case someone came in and saw us together, even though we were doing nothing but sitting side by side on the edge of the mosaic 'platform' with our feet dangling, like two kids sitting on a wall. But at least we could be pretty sure no white man or woman would come into the gardens. They never did. The gardens always seemed to have a purely Indian connection, just as the maiden really had a purely English one.

PAUL SCOTT, The Jewel in the Crown, (1966)

Bugs are not going to inherit the earth. They own it now. So, we might as well make peace with the landlord.

THOMAS EISNER, entomologist

POINT OF INTEREST

In the grounds of Holwood House, is a stone seat where William Pitt the Younger was accustomed to sitting and discussing political issues with fellow MPs when he was Prime Minister in the 1780s. Indeed, it was on this bench that Tory MP and anti-slave trade campaigner William Wilberforce announced to Pitt his resolve to bring an end to the slave trade. Overlooking the seat was a grand old oak tree that subsequently became known as the Wilberforce Oak, in memory of Wilberforce's convictions. Sadly, the original oak has succumbed to old age, but in 1952, an oak sapling was planted among the remains of the old tree in continual recognition of Wilberforce's achievement.

The best place to find God is in a garden.

You can dig for him there.

GEORGE BERNARD SHAW, playwright

Hamlet's father's ghost tells Hamlet how he was murdered by his brother, Hamlet's uncle, by a poisonous plant.

> Sleeping within mine orchard,
> My custom always in the afternoon,
> Upon my secure hour thy uncle stole
> With juice of cursed hebenon in a vial,
> And in the porches of mine ears did pour
> The leperous distilment; whose effect
> Holds such an enmity with blood of man,
> That, swift as quicksilver, it courses through
> The natural gates and alleys of the body;
> And with a sudden vigour it doth posset
> And curd, like eager droppings into milk,
> The thin and wholesome blood: so, did it mine;
> And a most instant tetter bark'd about,
> Most lazar-like, with vile and loathsome crust,
> All smooth body.

HAMLET, (Act 1 Scene 5) William Shakespeare, (1599)

It is a blessed sort of work, and if Eve had had a spade in Paradise and known what to do with it, we should not have had all that sad business of the apple.

ELIZABETH VON ARNIM, countess and author

POINT OF INTEREST

Henry II created a garden for his wife, Eleanor of Aquitaine, at Winchester and a romantic bower for his mistress, Rosamund Clifford, at Woodstock. The bower was a grand affair with three cottages and a water garden fed by a spring. Word of the bower quickly spread, starting a trend for Rosamund bowers throughout the country. But the popularity of Henry and Rosamund's love garden may well have been poor Rosamund's undoing – rumour has it that when word of the garden reached Eleanor's ear, she had Henry's mistress murdered. When hearing of her death, the poor King Henry II was apparently so full of despair that he ordered she be disinterred so that he could say a final goodbye.

The earth delights to feel your bare feet

and the winds long to play with your hair.

KHALIL GIBRAN, author

PAUSE FOR THOUGHT

Iago: Virtue? a fig! 'Tis in ourselves that we are thus or thus. Our bodies are our gardens, to the which our wills are gardeners: so that if we will plant nettles, or sow lettuce, set hyssop and weed up thyme, supply it with one gender of herbs, or distract it with many, either to have it sterile with idleness, or manured with industry, why, the power and corrigible authority of this lies in our wills.

WILLIAM SHAKESPEARE, Othello, The Moor of Venice, Act I, Scene 3, (1603)

He who plants a tree plants a hope.

LUCY LARCOM, poet

POINT OF INTEREST

British summers are getting hotter and hotter, and the English cottage garden is now under threat from the effects of global warming, according to a joint Royal Horticultural Society (RHS) and National Trust report. According to the report, our gardens are already suffering from global warming and within the next 50–80 years, we could start finding it difficult to maintain the healthy, green lawns England is known for. Concerning weather trends include fewer frosts, increased winter rainfall and flood risks, earlier springs, higher than average yearly temperatures, and hotter, drier summers with risks of drought.

These weather patterns could provide major challenges to gardeners seeking to maintain and preserve cold-climate plants. And, although the longer growing season would provide greater opportunities to grow exotic fruits, the water-logged winters might kill off many

Mediterranean species which dislike excess water. The warmer weather may also enable garden pests to survive winters, allowing them to attack plants when they are at their most vulnerable.

The earth laughs at him who calls a place his own.

GARDEN PROVERB

Every garden has its own particular feature, something unique, which is its focus and its strength, and which gives it its character and distinguishes it from every other garden. It may be its situation or shape or a certain aspect or vista within it, or else something individual – a tree or shrub, unusual or fine, an archway, a gate, an old wall, a summerhouse, a perfect lawn. You have only to discover and recognise that individuality, and allow it to express itself, or at least, do nothing to destroy or detract from it. Like the charm of a person, it may not be revealed to you at once, or even for a year or more, but if you live in humble and expectant mood with a garden, in the course of time you will come to know it. And if you begin with a bare and muddy acre, unplanted, unshaped, then you can help to mould the character of the garden to yourself.

SUSAN HILL, Through the Garden Gate, (1986)

May I a small house and garden have;

and a few friends too, and many books

both true.

ABRAHAM COWLEY, poet

POINT OF INTEREST

Tomatoes originated in South America. They were 'discovered' in 1550 by Spanish settlers in Mexico and brought back to Spain from where they quickly spread around Europe. In France, they became known as 'pomme d'amour' (apple of love) acquiring a risqué reputation as an aphrodisiac and in England, where they were also known as 'love apples', they were only grown as decorative plants that were whispered about.

The Earth is a large garden, and each of us need only care for our own part of life to be breathed back into the planet, into the soil, into ourselves.

JOHN JEAVONS, author and ecologist

Very often, last summer, I felt just like that. What happiness it is to work from dawn to dusk for your family and yourself, to build a roof over their head, to till the soil to feed them, to create your own world, like Robinson Crusoe, in imitation of the Creator of the universe and to bring forth your life, as if you were your own mother, again and again. So many new thoughts come into your head when your hands are busy with hard physical work, when your mind has set you a task which can be achieved by physical effort and which brings its reward in joy and success, when for six hours on end you dig or hammer, scorched by the life-giving breath of the sky. And it isn't a loss but a gain that these transient thoughts, intuitions, analogies, are not put down on paper but forgotten.

BORIS PASTERNAK, Doctor Zhivago, (1956)

A book is like a garden carried in the pocket.

GARDEN PROVERB

POINT OF INTEREST

In the late 1940s Edward James, an English traveller on his way to Mexico City stopped off for a rest in a forest just outside a monastry at Xilitla. Edward was apparently looking up at the sky, when a cloud of butterflies descended, blocking out the light of the sun. This inspired him to build a public garden in the middle of the forest, and the resulting gardens, Las Pozas, are a delicate fantasy of towering colonnades, impossibly elaborate fountains, doors that appear to be entrances but are actually exits and staircases that lead to the sky. This lost world fantasy has become quickly populated with colonising vines and epiphytes that are devouring the dreamy architecture and returning it slowly back to jungle.

BLOOMING
MARVELLOUS

Under the sweet-peas I stood
And drew deep breaths. They smelt so good.
Then, with strange enchanted eyes,
I saw them change to butterflies.
Higher than the skylark sings
I saw their fluttering crimson wings
Leave their garden-trellis bare
And fly into the upper air.
Standing in an elfin trance
Through the clouds I saw them glance...
Then I stretched my hand up high
And touched them in the distant sky.
At once the coloured wings came back
From wandering in the Zodiac.
Under the sweet-peas I stood
And drew deep breaths. They smelt so good.

ALFRED NOYES, A Child's Vision

From the orchard across the way the smell of ripe pears floats over the child's bed. A band rehearses waltzes in the distance. White things gleam in the dark – white flowers and paving stones. The moon on the window panes careens to the garden and ripples the succulent exhalations of the earth like a silver paddle. The world is younger than it is, and she to herself appears so old and wise, grasping her problems and wrestling with them as affairs peculiar to herself and not as racial heritages. There is a brightness and bloom over things; she inspects life proudly, as if she walked in a garden forced by herself to grow in the least hospitable of soils. She is already contemptuous of ordered planting, believing in the possibility of a wizard cultivator to bring forth sweet smelling blossoms from the hardest of rocks, and night-blooming vines from barren wastes, to plant the breath of twilight and to shop with marigolds. She wants life to be easy and full of pleasant reminiscences.

ZELDA FITZGERALD, Save me the Waltz, (1932)

To be overcome by the fragrance of flowers is a delectable form of defeat.

BEVERLEY NICHOLS, author

POINT OF INTEREST

Flowers in wedding bouquets are frequently chosen for their symbolism as well as colour and fragrance. A bouquet of daisies, ivy and lily represents innocence, fidelity and purity, while roses and orange blossom denote passionate love and fertility.

Earth laughs in flowers.

RALPH WALDO EMERSON, essayist

However, there was the hill full in sight, so there was nothing to be done but start again. This time she came upon a large flower-bed, with a border of daisies, and a willow-tree growing in the middle.

'O Tiger-lily!' said Alice, addressing herself to one that was waving gracefully about in the wind, 'I wish you could talk!' 'We can talk!' said the Tigerlily, 'when there's anybody worth talking to.' Alice was so astonished that she couldn't speak for a minute: it quite seemed to take her breath away. At length, as the Tigerlily only went on waving about, she spoke again, in a timid voice – almost in a whisper. 'And can all the flowers talk?' 'As well as you can,' said the Tiger-lily. 'And a great deal louder.' 'It isn't manners for us to begin, you know,' said the Rose, 'and I really was wondering when you'd speak! Said I to myself, Her face has got some sense in it, though it's not a clever one! Still, you're the right colour, and that goes a long way.' 'I don't care about the colour,' the Tiger-lily remarked. 'If only her petals curled up a little more, she'd be all right.' Alice didn't like being criticised, so she began asking questions. 'Aren't you sometimes frightened at being planted out here, with nobody to take care of you?' 'There's the tree in the middle,' said the Rose. 'What else is it good for?' 'But what could it do, if any danger came?' Alice asked. 'It could bark,' said the Rose. 'It says "Boughwough!"' cried a Daisy. 'That's

why its branches are called boughs!' 'Didn't you know that?' cried another Daisy. And here they all began shouting together, till the air seemed quite full of little shrill voices. 'Silence, every one of you!' cried the Tiger-lily, waving itself passionately from side to side, and trembling with excitement. 'They know I can't get at them!' it panted, bending its quivering head towards Alice, 'or they wouldn't dare to do it!' 'Never mind!' Alice said in a soothing tone, and, stooping down to the daisies, who were just beginning again, she whispered 'If you don't hold your tongues, I'll pick you!' There was silence in a moment, and several of the pink daisies turned white. 'That's right!' said the Tigerlily. 'The daisies are worst of all. When one speaks, they all begin together, and it's enough to make one wither to hear the way they go on!'

'How is it you can all talk so nicely?' Alice said, hoping to get it into a better temper by a compliment. 'I've been in many gardens before, but none of the flowers could talk.'

LEWIS CARROLL, Alice Through the Looking Glass, (1871)

The rose has thorns only for those who would gather it.

CHINESE PROVERB

POINT OF INTEREST

Roses became an important emblem during Henry VII's marriage to Elizabeth when a rose bush growing in Wiltshire started flowering with mottled red and white blooms. The Tudors adopted it as their symbol in order to unite the houses of York (traditionally a white rose) and Lancaster (traditionally a red rose).

Classified as Rosa x damascene var versicolor, the mottled red and white rose is still grown today.

In Flanders fields the poppies blow

Between the crosses, row on row.

JOHN MCCRAE, soldier

Cordelia: Alack! 'tis he: why, he was met even now As mad as the vex'd sea; singing aloud; Crown'd with rank fumiter and furrow weeds, With burdocks, hemlock, nettles, cuckoo-flowers, Darnel, and all the idle weeds that grow In our sustaining corn. A century sends forth; Search every acre in the high-grown field And bring him to our eye.

WILLIAM SHAKESPEARE, King Lear, Act IV, Scene 6, (1606)

Don't worry about the future; better laze under the trees, drinking wine and making fragrant our graying locks with roses.

HORACE, poet

POINT OF INTEREST

In 1542, Leonhart Fuchs established the Latin name *digitalis* for the plant we now know as the foxglove. *Digitalis* means finger in Latin, and the plant was apparently named so because it was known in some parts of England as the finger-flower, whose petals resemble the fingers of a brightly-coloured glove whose ends had been snipped off. But this plant's distinctively shaped flowers have also been called a variety of other names, each inspired by the image of little fingers, or little paws. The word foxglove itself is believed to have come from the term folk's glove, as the plant was thought to resemble the gloves of fairies. Some even knew it as fairy fingers, and in one particularly charming variation, it was known as fox fingers because it was thought the flowers were worn by foxes to keep the dew off their paws.

The love of gardening is a seed once sown that never dies.

GERTRUDE JEKYLL, horticulturalist

It was the sweetest, most mysterious-looking place anyone could imagine. The high walls which shut it in were covered with the leafless stems of climbing roses which were so thick that they were matted together. Mary Lennox knew they were roses because she had seen a great many roses in India. All the ground was covered with grass of a wintry brown and out of it grew clumps of bushes which were surely rosebushes if they were alive. There were numbers of standard roses which had so spread their branches that they were like little trees. There were other trees in the garden, and one of the things which made the place look strangest and loveliest was that climbing roses had run all over them and swung down long tendrils which made light swaying curtains, and here and there they had caught at each other or at a far-reaching branch and had crept from one tree to another and made lovely bridges of themselves. There were neither leaves nor roses on them now and Mary did not know whether they were dead or alive, but their thin gray or brown branches and sprays looked like a sort of hazy mantle spreading over everything, walls, and trees, and even brown grass, where they had fallen from their fastenings and run along the ground. It was this hazy tangle from tree to tree which made it all look so mysterious. Mary had thought it must be different from other gardens which had not

been left all by themselves so long; and indeed it was different from any other place she had ever seen in her life.

FRANCES HODGSON BURNETT, The Secret Garden, (1911)

Gardens are not made by sitting in the shade.

RUDYARD KIPLING, author

POINT OF INTEREST

Fleur-de-lys

This familiar design is a stylised representation of the 'fleur de luce', the common wild iris that grows in swamps. According to legend, the 6th century French King Clovis faced death when his retreat from battle was cut off by a river. By tracing his way through wild iris, his army followed a shallow route to safety, and in gratitude, he adopted the flower as his emblem.

Gardening is the slowest of performing arts.

ANONYMOUS

As spring came on, a new set of amusements became the fashion, and the lengthening days gave long afternoons for work and play of all sorts. The garden had to be put in order, and each sister had a quarter of the little plot to do what she liked with. Hannah used to say, 'I'd know which each of them gardings belonged to, ef I see 'em in Chiny,' and so she might, for the girls' tastes differed as much as their characters. Meg's had roses and heliotrope, myrtle, and a little orange tree in it. Jo's bed was never alike two seasons, for she was always trying experiments. This year it was to be a plantation of sun flowers, the seeds of which cheerful and aspiring plant were to feed Aunt Cockle-top and her family of chicks. Beth had old-fashioned fragrant flowers in her garden, sweet peas and mignonette, larkspur, pinks, pansies, and southernwood, with chickweed for the birds and catnip for the pussies. Amy had a bower in hers, rather small and earwiggy, but very pretty to look at, with honeysuckle and morning-glories hanging their colored horns and bells in graceful wreaths all over it, tall white lilies, delicate ferns, and as many brilliant, picturesque plants as would consent to blossom there.

LOUISA MAY ALCOTT, Little Women, (1868)

More than anything, I must have flowers always, always.

CLAUDE MONET, artist

POINT OF INTEREST

Native to the Sumatran rainforests, the corpse flower has the dubious reputation of being not only the world's biggest (it can grow to six feet tall) but also the world's smelliest flower, with a smell that mimics that of rotting flesh in order to attract the carrion beetle that pollinates the flower. It is also a plant under threat in the wild and attempts to propagate it in the laboratory have proved very difficult; not least because it can take up to 15 years to flower, and male and female parts do not mature at the same time (making self-pollination impossible). Fortunately, Huntingdon Botanical Gardens in California successfully created a technique to pollinate the plant using a bag of rotten apples in 2000. The rotten apples produced ethylene gas, which encouraged the flowers to ripen early and allowed the plants to self-pollinate.

PLANT LORE

Just now the lilac is in bloom,
All before my little room;
And in my flower-beds, I think,
Smile the carnation and the pink;
And down the borders, well I know,
The poppy and the pansy blow...
Oh! there the chestnuts, summer through,
Beside the river make for you
A tunnel of green gloom, and sleep
Deeply above; and green and deep
The stream mysterious glides beneath,
Green as a dream and deep as death.
– Oh, damn! I know it! and I know
How the May fields all golden show,
And when the day is young and sweet,
Gild gloriously the bare feet
That run to bathe...

RUPERT BROOK, The Old Vicarage, Grantchester

So the Brangwens came and went without fear of necessity, working hard because of the life that was in them, not for want of the money. Neither were they thriftless. They were aware of the last halfpenny, and instinct made them not waste the peeling of their apple, for it would help to feed the cattle. But heaven and earth was teeming around them, and how should this cease? They felt the rush of the sap in spring, they knew the wave which cannot halt, but every year throws forward the seed to begetting, and, falling back, leaves the young-born on the earth. They knew the intercourse between heaven and earth, sunshine drawn into the breast and bowels, the rain sucked up in the daytime, nakedness that comes under the wind in autumn, showing the birds' nests no longer worth hiding. Their life and interrelations were such; feeling the pulse and body of the soil...

DH LAWRENCE, The Rainbow, (1915)

One for the rock, one for the crow,

One to die and one to grow.

ANON

POINT OF INTEREST

The spice saffron comes – surprise, surprise – from the saffron crocus. Indeed, the word crocus comes from the Greek word for saffron – *krokos*. Few gardeners cultivate the saffron crocus, which is a sorry looking plant that is prone to disease. Saffron is believed to have been introduced into England by the Romans and by the time of Henry VIII, it was being used to dye the royal sheets as an antiseptic. In the 17th century, there was a great industry of saffron at Saffron Walden, but much of today's saffron now comes from Iran. Each saffron crocus has three stigmas and it takes about 4,400 stigmas to make an ounce of saffron.

God Almighty first planted a garden. And Indeed it is the purest of human pleasures.

FRANCIS BACON, English philosopher and statesman

April 8, Sunday. — After Church, the Curate came back with us. I sent Carrie in to open front door, which we do not use except on special occasions. She could not get it open, and after all my display, I had to take the Curate (whose name, by-the-by, I did not catch,) round the side entrance. He caught his foot in the scraper, and tore the bottom of his trousers. Most annoying, as Carrie could not well offer to repair them on a Sunday. After dinner, went to sleep. Took a walk round the garden, and discovered a beautiful spot for sowing mustard-and-cress and radishes. Went to Church again in the evening: walked back with the Curate. Carrie noticed he had got on the same pair of trousers, only repaired. He wants me to take round the plate, which I think a great compliment.

GEORGE GROSSMITH, The Diary of a Nobody, (1892)

Tickle it with a hoe and it will laugh into a harvest.

GARDEN PROVERB

POINT OF INTEREST

Black hellebore leaves were reputedly used by witches for charms and spells. So evil were its leaves, that even collecting this plant was considered a dangerous task. According to the natural historian, Pliny the Elder, gatherers had to draw a circle round the plant with a sword and seek permission from the gods to lift the plant from the ground. Gatherers were also advised to look east and avoid being witnessed by an eagle for if they were, they might die within a year.

The greatest service which can be rendered to any country is to add a useful plant to its culture.

THOMAS JEFFERSON, former US president

AMARA DULCIS:

Considering divers shires in this nation give divers names to one and the same herb, and that the common name which it bears in one county, is not known in another; I shall take the pains to set down all the names that I know of each herb: pardon me for setting that name first, which is most common to myself. Besides Amara Dulcis, some call it Mortal, others Bitter-sweet; some Woody Night-shade, and others Felon-wort.

DESCRIPTION - It grows up with woody stalks even to a man's height, and sometimes higher. The leaves fall off at the approach of winter, and spring out of the same stalk at spring-time: the branch is compassed about with a whitish bark, and has a pith in the middle of it: the main branch branches itself into many small ones with claspers, laying hold on what is next to them, as vines do: it bears many leaves, they grow in no order at all, at least in no regular order; the leaves are longish, though somewhat broad, and pointed at the ends: many of them have two little leaves growing at the end of their foot-stalk; some have but one, and some none. The leaves are of a pale green colour; the flowers are of a purple colour, or of a perfect blue, like to violets, and they stand many of them together in knots: the berries are green

at first, but when they are ripe they are very red; if you taste them, you shall find them just as the crabs which we in Sussex call Bittersweet, viz. sweet at first and bitter afterwards.

Government and virtues. It is under the planet Mercury, and a notable herb of his also, if it be rightly gathered under his influence. It is excellently good to remove witchcraft both in men and beasts, as also all sudden diseases whatsoever. Being tied round about the neck, is one of the most admirable remedies for the vertigo or dizziness in the head; and that is the reason (as Tragus saith) the people in Germany commonly hang it about their cattle's necks, when they fear any such evil hath betided2 them: Country people commonly take the berries of it, and having bruised them, apply them to felons, and thereby soon rid their fingers of such troublesome guests.

NICHOLAS CULPEPPER, The Complete Herbal, (1852)

True Friendship is a plant of small growth.

GEORGE WASHINGTON, former US President

POINT OF INTEREST

At least 300 million years old, cycads are one of the earth's oldest plants. Known for their large attractive palm-like leaves, there are about 300 different species and sub-species of cycads in Asia, Africa, the Americas and Australia, but an astonishing 53% of them are threatened with extinction.

One of the problems is that these plants grow very slowly and depend on specialist pollinators. In one subspecies, the plants' natural pollinator no longer exists, and pollination is done artificially.

They are suffering from habitat destruction, urban development, invasive plant species and collection for horticulture and landscaping. To discourage their collection from the wild, scientists have developed a unique method to tell if the cycads available for the garden are wild or cultivated using microchips and DNA-tracing techniques.

We sow with all the art we know

and not a plant appears.

A single seed from any weed a

thousand children rears.

ANON

PAUSE FOR THOUGHT

Harris asked me if I'd ever been in the maze at Hampton Court. He said he went in once to show somebody else the way. He had studied it on a map, and it was so simple that it seemed foolish – hardly worth the two pence charged for admission. He said 'We'll just go in here, so that you can say you've been, but it's very simple. It's absurd to call it a maze. You keep on taking the first turning to the right. We'll just walk round for ten minutes and then go and get some lunch.'

They met some people soon after they had got inside, who said they'd been there for three quarters of an hour and had had about enough of it. Harris told them they could follow him if they liked; he was just going in, and then would turn around and go out again. They said it was very kind of him and fell behind and followed.

They picked up various other people who wanted to get it over as they went along, until they absorbed all the persons in the maze. People who had given up all hopes of ever getting in or out, or of ever seeing their home and friends again, plucked up their courage at the sight of Harris and his party, and joined the procession, blessing him... Harris kept on turning to the right, but it seemed a long way, and his cousin said he supposed it was a very big maze.

'Oh, one of the largest in Europe,' said Harris.

'Yes, it must be,' replied the cousin, 'because we've walked a good two miles already.'

JEROME K JEROME, Three Men in a Boat, (1889)

He that planteth a tree is a servant of God, he provideth a kindness for many generations, and faces that he hath not seen shall bless him.

HENRY VAN DYKE, author

POINT OF INTEREST

Saponin is the chemical responsible for producing the frothy lather in soap. Plants that contain saponin include:

- Soapwort, a European herbaceous perennial whose leaves produce a green lather when rubbed or boiled in water.

- Balinites aegyptiaca, a spiny tree that grows in Sudan and Chad, and was used in ancient Egypt. It contains an edible oil, which also makes a foaming soap.

- The soap tree, which originated in Chile. Its bark is used as both a soap and a foaming agent for drinks.

- The lac trees. Oil from its seeds is used as a hair oil. It was a popular remedy for gentlemen during the Victorian times, when it was known as Madagascar oil.

I wanted said of me by those who knew me best that I always plucked a thistle and planted a flower where I thought a flower would grow.

ABRAHAM LINCOLN, former US president

The Greek philosopher Socrates died in 399 BC in Athens after being forced to drink the poison colchicines, which is derived from the spotted hemlock plant, which grows near rivers, streams, hedges and some gardens in Britain. Socrates had been condemned to death after a state sponsored trial, which found him guilty of impiety, heresy and corrupting the youth of Athens. His trial, stubborn defence and painful death were witnessed by friends and written up by Plato:

Then holding the cup to his lips, quite readily and cheerfully he drank off the poison. And hitherto most of us had been able to control our sorrow; but now when we saw him drinking, and saw too that he had finished the draught, we could no longer forbear, and in spite of myself my own tears were flowing fast; so that I covered my face and wept over myself, for certainly I was not weeping over him, but at the thought of my own calamity in having lost such a companion. Nor was I the first, for Crito, when he found himself unable to restrain his tears, had got up and moved away, and I followed; and at that moment, Apollodorus, who had been weeping all the time, broke out into a loud cry which made cowards of us all. Socrates alone retained his calmness: What is this strange outcry? he said. I sent away the women mainly in order that they might not

offend in this way, for I have heard that a man should die in peace. Be quiet, then, and have patience.

The death of Socrates from Plato's Phaedo, translated by BENJAMIN JOWETT, (1871)

Science, or para-science, tells us that geraniums bloom better if they are spoken to. But a kind word every now and then is really quite enough. Too much attention, like too much feeding, and weeding and hoeing, inhibits and embarrasses them.

VICTORIA GLENDINNING, author

POINT OF INTEREST

Fourth century AD Chinese civil servant and poet, Ton Guen-ming is thought to have dreamt up the idea of the Chinese penjing (tray garden).

Penjing is the predecessor to bonsai growing, which itself widely thought of as Japanese, was brought to Japan from China by Buddhist monks in 1195 AD.

POTPOURRI

The little fires that Nature lights –
The scilla's lamp, the daffodil –
She quenches, when of stormy nights
Her anger whips the hill.
The fires she lifts against the cloud –
The irised bow, the burning tree –
She batters down with curses loud,
Nor cares that death should be.
The fire she kindles in the soul –
The poet's mood, the rebel's thought –
She cannot master, for their coal
In other mines is wrought

JOSEPH CAMPBELL, Fires

The garden that is finished is dead.

H.E. BATES, author

POINT OF INTEREST

The first gardening tools were believed to have been constructed about 40,000 years ago from animal bones. Mattocks were made from sheep's horns, tied to sticks; dibbers were constructed out of mammoth's ribs; and shovels were made from the shoulder blades of oxen.

To forget how to dig the earth and to tend the soil is to forget ourselves.

MAHATMA GANDHI, statesman

PAUSE FOR THOUGHT

I walked a while on the pavement; but a subtle, well-known scent — that of a cigar — stole from some window; I saw the library casement open a handbreadth; I knew I might be watched thence; so I went apart into the orchard. No nook in the grounds more sheltered and more Eden-like; it was full of trees, it bloomed with flowers: a very high wall shut it out from the court, on one side; on the other, a beech avenue screened it from the lawn. At the bottom was a sunk fence; its sole separation from lonely fields: a winding walk, bordered with laurels and terminating in a giant horse-chestnut, circled at the base by a seat, led down to the fence.

Here one could wander unseen. While such honey-dew fell, such silence reigned, such gloaming gathered, I felt as if I could haunt such shade for ever; but in threading the flower and fruit parterres at the upper part of the enclosure, enticed there by the light the now rising moon cast on this more open quarter, my step is stayed — not by sound, not by sight, but once more by a warning fragrance.

Sweet-briar and southernwood, jasmine, pink, and rose have long been yielding their evening sacrifice of incense: this new scent is neither of shrub nor flower; it is — I know it well — it is Mr.

Rochester's cigar. I look round and I listen. I see trees laden

with ripening fruit. I hear a nightingale warbling in a wood half a mile off; no moving form is visible, no coming step audible; but that perfume increases: I must flee. I make for the wicket leading to the shrubbery, and I see Mr. Rochester entering. I step aside into the ivy recess; he will not stay long: he will soon return whence he came, and if I sit still he will never see me.

CHARLOTTE BRONTË, Jayne Eyre, (1847)

There's one good thing about snow, it makes your lawn look as nice as your neighbour's.

CLYDE MOORE, gardener

POINT OF INTEREST

This was the question posed by John Jeavons, an American gardener with a passion for preserving goodness in the soil. In the 1970s, he devised a three-section mini-farm, dividing one section for food crops, one for compost crops and one for income-generation crops. His garden yielded at least twice as many (and sometimes 15 times as many) vegetables as the American national average and his experiment has been adopted by gardeners throughout the world.

Gardening adds years to your life and life to your years.

ANONYMOUS

I admit that Versailles, Courances and Villandry are superb achievements of the architectural school of gardening. Yet a garden is intended for the pleasure of its owner and not for ostentation. Nobody could sit with his family on the parterre of Versailles and read the Sunday papers while sipping China tea. Nobody who really cares for flowers can really want them arranged in patterns as if they were carpets from Shiraz or Isfahan. Most civilised people prefer the shade of some dear family tree to the opulence of a parterre, displaying its patter under the wide-open sky.

HAROLD NICHOLSON, gardener and politician in the introduction to Great Gardens of Britain by Peter Coats, (1967)

A perfect summer day is when the sun is shining,the breeze is blowing, the birds are singing,and the lawn mower is broken.

JAMES DENT, humourist

POINT OF INTEREST

Although modern toothbrushes with nylon bristles are a western invention that dates back to the 1930s, the toothbrush story goes as far back as 5,000 years, when Egyptians used small tree branches with frayed ends to ensure their dental hygiene. Europe imported the idea in the 15th century from China, where locals were using the neck hair of Siberian wild boar mounted on bamboo handles. But for centuries people have used parts of plants to clean their teeth – and still do. In East Africa, sticks from the *Diospyros* tree are popular natural toothbrushes, and have recently been found to contain anti-fungal properties. In the Middle East and India, the sticks of a tree unsurprisingly known as the toothbrush tree are chewed for their juice, which has been found to contain an anti-bacterial compound. And in Burma, locals chew a mixture of charcoal and salt – which apparently makes the teeth very white!

Life begins the day you start a garden.

CHINESE PROVERB

The Weatherbury bees were late in their swarming this year. It was in the latter part of June, and the day after the interview with Troy in the hayfield, that Bathsheba was standing in her garden, watching a swarm in the air and guessing their probable settling place. Not only were they late this year, but unruly. Sometimes throughout a whole season all the swarms would alight on the lowest attainable bough - such as part of a currant-bush or espalier apple-tree; next year they would, with just the same unanimity, make straight off to the uppermost member of some tall, gaunt costard, or quarrenden, and there defy all invaders who did not come armed with ladders and staves to take them.

This was the case at present. Bathsheba's eyes, shaded by one hand, were following the ascending multitude against the unexplorable stretch of blue till they ultimately halted by one of the unwieldy trees spoken of. A process somewhat analogous to that of alleged formations of the universe, time and times ago, was observable. The bustling swarm had swept the sky in a scattered and uniform haze, which now thickened to a nebulous centre: this glided on to a bough and grew still denser, till it formed a solid black spot upon the light.

THOMAS HARDY, Far from the Madding Crowd, (1874)

A society grows great when old men plant trees whose shade they know they shall never sit in.

GREEK PROVERB

POINT OF INTEREST

Jan van der Heide invented the standard leather garden hose in 1672. Not until the mid-19th century was it updated. British chemist, Henry Bewley was the first to manufacture garden hoses out of gutta percha (a natural material similar to rubber from Malaysia). In the mid-20th century, gutta percha was also used to cover transatlantic cables, which just goes to prove that all the best things come out of the garden.

Flowers always make people better, happier, and more helpful; they are sunshine, food and medicine for the soul.

LUTHER BURBANK, botanist

It will never rain roses: when we want more roses we must plant more trees.

GEORGE ELIOT, author

POINT OF INTEREST

Take a handful of soil that is slightly moist and crush it in the palm of your hand. If the soil keeps the impressions of your fingers it's clay, if it crumbles immediately it's sand, but if it holds its shape briefly and then crumbles into small chunks, it's loam.

A weed is but an unloved flower.

ELLA WHEELER WILCOX, author

The Minister's answer was to let out a burp, which I considered a very well-spoken reply because it was apparent, he was about to throw up. Nobu and I rushed over to help him, but he'd already clamped his hand over his mouth. If he'd been a volcano, he would have been smoking by this time, so we had no choice but to roll open the glass doors to the garden to let him vomit onto the snow there. You may be appalled at the thought of a man throwing up into one of these exquisite decorative gardens, but the Minister certainly wasn't the first. We geisha try to help a man down the hallway to the toilet, but sometimes we can't manage it. If we say to one of the maids that a man has just visited the garden, they all know exactly what we mean and come at once with their cleaning supplies.

ARTHUR GOLDEN, Memoirs of a Geisha, (1997)

The soul cannot thrive in the absence of a garden.

SIR THOMAS MOORE, statesman and philosopher

POINT OF INTEREST

Mint's origins in Europe can be traced all the way back to Greek mythology. This wonderfully fragrant herb is named after Minthe, a nymph who won the affections of Pluto, a mighty God and coincidentally a mighty philanderer. To prevent his wife's revenge, he transformed Minthe into an herb.

Mint's historical uses are countless; its health benefits undeniable.

Hebrews laid it on synagogue floors for disguising unpleasant smells.

Romans flavoured their wines and sauces with it. Mixed with honey into a refreshing paste, it was used by ladies to mask secret wine sipping, a crime charged with the death penalty in ancient Rome.

Mint can reduce flatulence, cure colds, unblock noses, prevent stomach ulcers, kill bacteria and reduce herpes.

TRIGGER
The mental health & wellbeing publisher

We want to help you to not just survive but thrive ... one book at a time
Find out more about Trigger Publishing by visiting our website:
triggerpublishing.com
or join us on:
Twitter @**TriggerPub**
Facebook @**TriggerPub**
Instagram @**TriggerPub**

*Shaw*mind
Your Local Mental Health & Wellbeing Charity

A proportion of profits from the sale of all Trigger books
go to their sister charity Shaw Mind,
founded by Adam Shaw and Lauren Callaghan.
The charity aims to ensure that everyone has access
to mental health resources whenever they need them.
Find out more: **shawmindfoundation.org**
or join them on:
Twitter: @**Shaw_Mind**
Instagram: @**Shaw_Mind**
LinkedIn: @**shaw-mind**
FB: @**shawmindUK**

To grow this magical herb in your back garden, simply
pick your favourite out of 600 varieties, and make sure
its roots are contained within a pot, as both roots and
aroma tend to take over the garden!